W9-DGC-677

WATER FIREWORKS
Kitchen Experiment

By Meg Gaertner

Published by The Child's World®
1980 Lookout Drive • Mankato, MN 56003-1705
800-599-READ • www.childsworld.com

Photographs ©: Rick Orndorf, cover, 1, 14, 16, 17, 18, 19, 20,
21; Shutterstock Images, 5; Estudi Vaque/Shutterstock Images, 6;
Danny Iacob/Shutterstock Images, 7; iStockphoto, 9, 10, 12

ISBN 9781503825383
LCCN 2017959700

Printed in the United States of America
PA02378

Table of Contents

CHAPTER 1

Fun with Fireworks

Have you ever seen **fireworks**? Some fireworks are rockets. They make bright colors and fun shapes in the sky. People use them during holidays such as the Fourth of July.

These fireworks have **gunpowder** inside. Gunpowder is a black powder. It blows up when it **ignites** or catches on fire. To use a firework, an adult will light a **fuse** on fire. A fuse is a short string. It comes out of the base of the firework. Heat moves up the fuse. The gunpowder ignites.

It is easier to see fireworks at night. They are bright against the dark sky.

The fuse goes into the bottom of the firework.

It blows up and sends the firework into the sky.

Some **chemicals** are packed with the gunpowder. Chemicals are made of special sets of **atoms**. Different chemicals make the different colors in fireworks.

Fireworks come in many different shapes and colors.

There is a second fuse inside the firework. It burns slowly. This fuse leads to more gunpowder. Heat moves up the second fuse. The extra gunpowder ignites when the rocket is in the air. The chemicals inside the firework shoot in different patterns. This creates the colored lights you see in the sky. Fireworks that use gunpowder are dangerous. But we can make safe fireworks at home!

CHAPTER 2

Density

Picture a piece of paper. If you rip it, you will have two pieces. If you keep ripping, the pieces will get smaller and smaller. Atoms are the tiniest bits that things can be broken into. They are very tiny. We can only see them with special machines.

Atoms come together to form **molecules**. **Density** measures how packed the molecules are inside things. Things that are dense have many molecules. They are very close together. Things that are less dense have few molecules. The molecules are farther apart.

We can build models of molecules to look at their shapes.

Even a large group of helium balloons is less dense than air.

Something that is dense might be small but heavy. A rock is dense. Something that is not dense might be big and light. The air inside a balloon is not very dense. A balloon can be bigger than a rock. But it is also lighter. If a balloon floats, it is filled with **helium**. Helium is a gas that is even less dense than air.

You can mix things with different densities. But they do not come together! Things that are more dense sink. Things that are less dense float. This is why helium balloons rise into the sky.

TIP

Think of density like children in a classroom. Say there are two children in a room. This is not very dense. There is a lot of space between the children. Now picture a room filled with many children. The children have less space to move around. The group is much more dense.

Oil and water do not mix. It is easy to see their layers in a container.

The helium is less dense than the air. This is also why a rock will sink in a pool. The rock is denser than the water.

To make fireworks, you will mix water and oil. Water and oil do not mix well. Oil is less dense than water. It will float on top of the water.

Food coloring will mix well with water. Food coloring is made of water. Food coloring molecules will spread out in water. This will give the color for your fireworks.

CHAPTER 3

THE EXPERIMENT
Let's Make
Water Fireworks!

TIME TO FINISH: 5-10 minutes

5
10

MATERIALS LIST

2 clear glasses
1 cup (237 mL) warm tap water
3 tablespoons (45 mL) oil
food coloring, different colors
fork

1. Pour the water into one glass.
2. Pour the oil into the other glass.

3. Add two drops of each color of food coloring to the oil.

4. Slowly mix the oil and food coloring with a fork. You will see the food coloring break into smaller drops.

5. Add the oil and food coloring slowly to the glass of water. The oil will stay on top of the water.

TIP
Be very gentle when adding the oil to the water. If you add it too quickly, the coloring will mix with the water too early.

TIP
The oil stays at the top of the glass. Food coloring is denser than oil so it falls. The drops of food coloring mix with the water. The color spreads into the water. The drops look like fireworks.

6. Watch your fireworks!

Glossary

atoms (AT-uhms) Atoms are the tiny bits that make up everything. Atoms come together to form molecules.

chemicals (KEM-uh-kuhls) Chemicals are made of special sets of atoms. The colors of fireworks are made using different chemicals.

density (DEN-si-tee) Density measures how closely packed molecules are in something. Air has a low density.

fireworks (FIRE-wurks) Fireworks are rockets filled with gunpowder and chemicals. Fireworks blow up into pretty colors and shapes in the sky.

fuse (FYOOZ) A fuse is a short string that comes out of the base of a firework. An adult lights a fuse to ignite a firework.

gunpowder (GUHN-pow-dur) Gunpowder is a black powder that easily catches on fire. Gunpowder is used in fireworks.

helium (HEE-lee-uhm) Helium is a gas that is lighter than air. Helium balloons rise in the sky.

ignites (ig-NITES) Something ignites when it catches on fire. Gunpowder ignites inside a firework.

molecules (MOL-uh-kyools) Molecules are groups of different types of atoms. The air we breathe is made of molecules.

To Learn More

In the Library

Einhorn, Kama. *The Explosive Story of Fireworks!* New York, NY: Simon Spotlight, 2015.

Lawrence, Ellen. *Liquids and Solids*. New York, NY: Bearport, 2015.

Spalding, Maddie. *Celebrating the Fourth of July*. Mankato, MN: The Child's World, 2018.

On the Web

Visit our Web site for links about fireworks:
childsworld.com/links

Note to Parents, Teachers, and Librarians: We routinely verify our Web links to make sure they are safe and active sites. So encourage your readers to check them out!

Index

About the Author

Meg Gaertner is a children's book author and editor who lives in Minnesota. When not writing, she enjoys dancing and spending time outdoors.